Starting 'Henry V'

by
John Mannion

Series Editor
Eric Boagey

Published by HarperCollins*Publishers* Limited
77–85 Fulham Palace Road
Hammersmith
London
W6 8JB

www.**Collins**Education.com
On-line support for schools and colleges

© 2001 John Mannion and Eric Boagey
First published 2001

ISBN 0 00 323092 9

John Mannion and Eric Boagey assert their moral rights to be identified as the authors of this work.

British Library Cataloguing in Publication Data
A catalogue record for this publication is available from the British Library.

Acknowledgements
The following permissions to reproduce material are gratefully acknowledged:
Text: Collins Alexander Shakespeare edition of *Henry V* for the play extracts and references
Photos: The Bridgeman Art Library, p. 7; © Donald Cooper/Photo*stage*, pp. 12, 19, 40; © Clive Barda, PAL, p. 20; Ronald Grant Archive, pp. 24, 29, 31, 36.

Whilst every effort has been made both to contact the copyright holders and to give exact credit lines, this has not proved possible in every case.

Cover and internal artwork by Paul McCaffrey and Nigel Jordan
Cover design by Ken Vail Graphic Design
Internal design by Jordan Publishing Design
Commissioned by Helen Clark
Edited by Rachel Orme-Smith and Kim Richardson
Production by Katie Morris
Printed and bound by Imago in Singapore

You might also like to visit
www.**fireandwater**.co.uk
The book lover's website

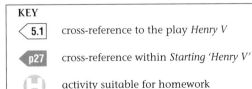

KEY

5.1   cross-reference to the play *Henry V*

p27   cross-reference within *Starting 'Henry V'*

   activity suitable for homework

Contents

Index of references to *Henry V*

Coverage of Assessment Objectives

Getting started

Ed and Ben have a chat about *Henry V*.

Ed   Let me ask you a question, Ben. Do you think *Henry V* – the play, I mean – is about English history?

Ben   Well, yes. It's about Henry winning the battle of Agincourt.

Ed   But is that all?

Ben   No, but that's the high point and that's history. The English did win, didn't they?

Ed   Yes, without doubt. But Shakespeare wrote to entertain an audience. And although he based the plot on Raphael Holinshed's *Chronicles of England, Scotland and Ireland* there's a lot in the play that is not straightforward history.

Ben   You mean the comedy?

Ed   Yes. In the comic scenes there isn't much history, but a lot of good theatrical entertainment for the audience at The Globe.

Ben   But we always come back to Henry. He dominates the play.

Ed   And what did you think of him?

Ben   I thought he was great. He wasn't pompous or arrogant. In fact, he seemed really humble at times. But clever, too. He knew how to handle people.

Ed   He was a good leader because he acted on principle and he really understood his men. Shakespeare makes him very human.

Ben   Like when he mixed with ordinary soldiers before the battle?

4.1 ▷

	Ed	Yes. You might think that he is a bit too perfect, but remember that Shakespeare was deliberately writing a patriotic play and Henry had to represent the finest qualities of a king.
	Ben	It's patriotic all right, but isn't it also a pro-war play?
	Ed	It doesn't glorify war. I think it gives a very realistic picture of war at that time. And it's still happening in the twenty-first century. Now we see it on television. Then it needed a Shakespeare to describe it.
⟨ 4.1 ⟩ ⟨ 3.2 ⟩	**Ben**	And Williams describing the men whose legs and arms and heads had been chopped off in battle! I agreed with the Boy when he said he wished he was in an alehouse in London and would give all his fame 'for a pot of ale and safety'!
⟨ 2.Pr ⟩	**Ed**	He seems to put the other side of the picture that the Chorus gives when all the youth of England are on fire. Maybe they were – before they got to France! But what did you think of the Chorus? Was he a help?
⟨ 2.Pr ⟩ ⟨ 3.Pr ⟩ ⟨ 4.Pr ⟩ ⟨ 5.Pr ⟩	**Ben**	Yes, he's like a guide on a conducted tour. Now we're going from Hampton Court to Southampton, now we're told about the three traitors, then crossing the Channel to France, the siege of Harfleur, the night before Agincourt and then, after the victory, back to London where the citizens pour out to welcome him! I would have been lost without him!
⟨ 1.Pr ⟩ ⟨ 1.2 ⟩	**Ed**	I think it was a brilliant idea of Shakespeare's to have a Chorus. He's the link between the stage and the audience, explaining the action but standing outside it. He apologizes for the limitations of the stage and asks the audience: 'Gently to hear, kindly to judge, our play'. Did you judge it kindly?
	Ben	Yes, once we'd got through the Archbishop of Canterbury's long speeches.
⟨ 5.2 ⟩	**Ed**	They're always a bit of a problem in the theatre. But by the end of the play Shakespeare is highlighting the human rather than the political. In fact, the only part of the peace treaty with France that he emphasizes is the marriage of Henry and Katherine – a romantic ending that would send the audience away happy! What did you think of Henry's wooing, Ben?
	Ben	Clever – like his war speeches! He always finds the right words to get what he wants!

 Write... a dialogue with Ed

You may not have agreed with some of Ed's and Ben's opinions, or you may want to add some of your own. Write another dialogue between Ed and yourself to express your own view of the play.

Historical background

Henry V and history

The period of English history from 1377 to 1485 was one of instability and unrest. Two branches of the royal family (the houses of Lancaster and York) were battling for the crown in a feud that eventually erupted as the Wars of the Roses. Shakespeare wrote eight plays that follow one another chronologically and cover this turbulent period of English history. The plays focus on the reigns of five kings: Richard II, Henry IV, Henry V, Henry VI and Richard III.

Henry V (1413–1422) was an incredibly successful king: he managed to maintain stability at home and win victory abroad. At home Henry put down an attempted rebellion by the Yorkist opposition, which made the kingdom – and the house of Lancaster – stronger than ever. Henry's campaigns in France were equally successful; the battle of Agincourt in 1415 was the start of a series of victories against the French king, Charles VI. The effort of the campaign exhausted Henry, however, and he died of camp fever in France in 1422.

Henry V

This was also the time of the Hundred Years' War when England was laying claim to the crown and territory of France. Henry V's claim to the French throne was through his descent from Edward III – his great-grandfather. King Edward's mother was Isabella, daughter of the then king of France, Philip IV. Philip's three sons succeeded him, but they themselves had no sons, so the succession should have gone to their sister Isabella's son – Edward III of England. But the French barred him and chose another king. Henry V took up the challenge and claimed that he, being a descendant of Isabella, should rightfully be the king of France.

The French denied this claim, pointing to the so-called 'Salique' (or Salic) law, which said that the throne of France could not be inherited from the

1.2 ▷

female side. This seemed to bar both Edward and Henry, as the English claim was based on descent from Isabella. According to the Archbishop of Canterbury in Act 1 scene 2, however, the Salic law did not apply in France – only in a certain part of Germany where some French people had settled. So Henry could claim the throne after all!

1.2 *Discuss... Henry's claim to France*

1. Henry is cautious about starting a war with France. What else does Canterbury say to persuade him to pursue his claim?
2. Why is Canterbury so keen to persuade Henry to go to war?
3. Do you think this section has relevance for a modern audience, or was it more interesting to an Elizabethan audience?

Elizabethan England

Henry V was a very political play in its day; its themes and ideas were close to the heart of the Elizabethan public. There were several important parallels between the historical play and the Elizabethan present.

Elizabeth was a popular and successful queen who created strong patriotic feeling through her defeat of the attempted Spanish invasion (the Armada). The Elizabethan audience would have seen in *Henry V* a reflection of this success through the victories in France and the patriotic feelings it aroused. The Chorus acts as a kind of cheerleader for this response in the audience (see page 40).

p40

The Elizabethans believed in the idea of the divine right of kings to rule, which meant that to depose a king was a sin as well as a form of treason. Elizabeth had proved herself to be a strong ruler who gave the country political stability despite the threats of plots and rebellions. The character of Henry in Shakespeare's play was a timely reminder of the benefits that can come from a moral, religious and just monarch who had the support of his or her people and the loyalty of the nobility.

1.2 *Discuss... images of order*

The idea of a divinely ordered state in which everyone has his place and does his duty is shown through various images in Act 1 scene 2. Look at the Archbishop of Canterbury's speech beginning 'Therefore doth heaven divide...'.
1. What image does he use here?
2. What type of people are part of this ordered state?
3. What image does Exeter use in his speech just before Canterbury's?

The Elizabethan theatre

The diagram of The Globe theatre below will help you to imagine what it was like to go to a performance of *Henry V* in Shakespeare's day.

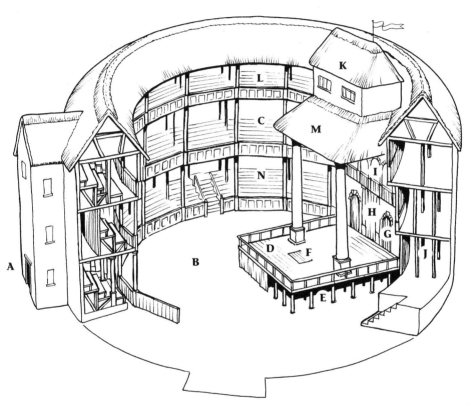

Key

A   Main entrance

B   The yard

C   Middle gallery

D   The stage

E   The area under the stage known as the 'Hell'

F   The stage trap, leading down to the Hell

G   Stage doors

H   Curtained alcove

I   Gallery above the stage, used as required by musicians, spectators, and as part of the play

J   Back-stage area (the tiring-house)

K   The hut housing the machinery for lowering thrones etc and where thunder and lightning effects were created

L   Upper gallery

M   The 'Heavens'

N   Lower gallery

The Globe theatre

It looks as though there wasn't any scenery.

1.Pr

No, just the back wall of the stage – two doors, a curtained alcove and the balcony. The balcony was an acting space, but it also included the musicians' gallery and 'the lords' room' where young gentlemen would sit. Shakespeare didn't bother too much about showing you the scene. The audience went to hear a play rather than to see one, and essential information is given in the dialogue or, in the case of *Henry V*, through the Chorus at the start of each act. In the prologue to Act 1 the Chorus draws attention to the contrast between the high theme of the play and the simplicity of the theatre:

> Can this cockpit hold
> The vasty fields of France? Or may we cram
> Within this wooden O the very casques
> That did affright the air at Agincourt?

Why is the Chorus only one actor? I thought a chorus was a group of people singing!

Good question! In classical Greek drama – which was beginning to influence the English theatre in the sixteenth century – the chorus was a group of actors, usually with a leader, who chanted and commented on the action of the play. Shakespeare uses the same idea and the same word, but with a single actor instead of a group – and no singing!

Shakespeare's acting company must have been pretty big – I've counted about forty-five characters in the play!

The company Shakespeare belonged to and wrote for was called the Lord Chamberlain's Men. It had about sixteen members, including boys. They managed to fill all the roles in *Henry V* by doubling (and sometimes trebling), so they had to be versatile!

Discuss... *staging and filming Henry V*

1. Do you think *Henry V* needs 'a cast of thousands' or could it be powerfully performed on a bare stage with a smallish cast?
2. What are the advantages of seeing *Henry V* on film rather than on the stage? Are there any disadvantages?

There are no stage battles in the play – unless you count the attack on Harfleur – so how did Shakespeare create the atmosphere of war?

3.1.2

I don't think he created an atmosphere in the modern sense. Sounds of war were created by firing actual small cannons and playing military music on trumpets and drums. The stage manager would have used properties (props) such as banners and scaling-ladders, but for the most part – as the Chorus says – the audience had to use its imagination, helped by Shakespeare's words.

1.Pr

 ## Discuss... *warfare in the theatre*

1. How would you create the impression of warfare on the modern stage? Here are some suggestions: using the beat of a drum, strobe lighting, projected images. Can you think of others?
2. Where would you use them in *Henry V*?

How much was it to get in?

A penny to stand in the yard, two pence for the middle gallery and another penny for the upper gallery. Sixpence for the lords' room overlooking the stage. Where would you go to see and hear best?

What about costumes? Did they use period dress?

No. They wore Elizabethan dress. But as there was no scenery, they made up for it by a lavish display of costumes, especially if the play contained royal and aristocratic characters, as our play does. But actors playing ordinary roles, such as Pistol and Bardolph, would have had to provide their own costumes.

Discuss... costumes

1. How would you dress a modern production of *Henry V*? Discuss costumes for nobles and soldiers, royalty and commoners.
2. Look at the photo below. Why do you think the director wanted a production in modern dress? Does a modern-dress production pose more problems than a period-dress production?

Did boys play the women's parts?

Yes. Women weren't allowed to act on the stage in Shakespeare's day. It was considered immoral! Boys – before their voices broke – acted all the women's roles. The boys playing Katherine and Alice in *Henry V* had not only to be convincing as women but to speak French as well!

 Discuss... male and female roles

In a single-sex class, who reads the male and female parts? In a mixed class, can boys read female parts as well as the girls? Or vice versa?

 Write... a letter

Imagine you are living in London in the early 1600s and you have just seen a performance of *Henry V* at The Globe. It is the first time you have been to the theatre. Write a letter to a friend who lives in the country, telling him or her what The Globe was like, and what you thought of the play.

The plot

In modern terms *Henry V* is a 'docu-drama'. It deals with real people and real events but it must also entertain its audience. What has Shakespeare done to keep his audience involved?

First of all, remind yourself of the play by looking through the brief summaries of each scene below.

Act 1

Prologue The Chorus introduces the play and its subject matter and expresses regret that such great events have to be played out on a small and inadequate stage.

1.1 The Archbishop of Canterbury and the Bishop of Ely discuss the re-introduction of a government bill which would transfer church land to the king. Canterbury hopes to distract Henry from the bill by offering him money to pursue his claim to the French throne.

1.2 Canterbury explains the legal basis of Henry's claim and urges war. Some of the nobles support this view. Henry decides to invade France. The French ambassadors bring an insulting present of tennis balls from the Dauphin. Henry is angry: he will reply with cannon balls.

Act 2

Prologue The Chorus describes the preparations for Henry's expedition and reveals that there is a conspiracy against him.

2.1 Bardolph, Pistol and Nym prepare for France. A fierce argument between Nym and Pistol breaks out because Pistol has married Nell Quickly (Hostess) to whom Nym was engaged. The Hostess enters and says that Sir John Falstaff is dying.

2.2 At Southampton Henry deals with a plot by trusted lords who took French bribes to kill him. The traitors admit their guilt and are condemned to death.

2.3 Falstaff has died and the Hostess, Pistol, Bardolph, Nym and the Boy recall moments in his life. They depart for France.

2.4 At the French court the French king is organizing the defence of France. The Dauphin is dismissive of the English threat, maintaining that Henry is a foolish youth; Constable disagrees. Exeter presents a demand that the French king accept Henry's claim to the throne and kingdom of France or there will be war.

Act 3

Prologue The Chorus now moves the scene of the play to France where the English have laid siege to Harfleur. The French offer of Princess Katherine and dukedoms has been rejected.

3.1 Henry makes a rousing speech encouraging his men to begin another attack upon Harfleur.

3.2 Pistol, Bardolph and Nym hang back, but are driven on by Fluellen. The Boy describes their true characters. Fluellen becomes involved in a dispute with Captains Macmorris (Irish), Jamy (Scottish) and Gower (English) about the 'disciplines of war'.

3.3 Henry addresses the citizens of Harfleur, describing the horrific consequences of not surrendering. The Governor surrenders. Henry resolves to retreat to Calais for the winter.

3.4 At the French court, Princess Katherine is given an English lesson by her maid.

3.5 The French nobles are dismayed at the English success. The king orders an army to be dispatched to fight the English and capture Henry.

3.6 Pistol reports that Bardolph is to be hanged for stealing from a church and pleads for clemency. Fluellen and Henry support the hanging. Henry orders his soldiers to show respect to the French villagers. Montjoy delivers a demand for Henry's surrender, which Henry rejects, in spite of the small size and ill-health of his army.

3.7 French nobles in their camp at Agincourt are impatient for battle and boast about the prisoners they will take.

Act 4

Prologue The Chorus describes the night before the battle of Agincourt and contrasts the over-confident French with the bedraggled English. Henry, however, is described going about encouraging his troops.

4.1 Henry in disguise walks about the English camp at night talking to his soldiers. Williams refuses to believe that the king will not allow himself to be ransomed (that is, to surrender and pay a ransom). He and Henry quarrel over this and agree to fight after the battle. They exchange gloves and agree to wear them in their caps in order to recognize each other. Henry delivers his soliloquy on 'ceremony' and offers up a prayer.

4.2 The arrogant French nobles are scornful of the sickly English as they make the final preparations for battle.

4.3 Henry makes an inspiring patriotic speech on the eve of St Crispin's day. Montjoy delivers a final demand for Henry's surrender and ransom. Henry rejects it.

4.4 A comic scene in which Pistol takes a prisoner.

4.5 The French nobles are in disorder but Bourbon leads them into battle again.

▶▶

4.6 The heroic deaths of Suffolk and York. When Henry realizes the French are gathering to attack again, he orders the prisoners to be killed.

4.7 Fluellen and Gower are shocked at the raid on the boys and the baggage and report Henry's decision to kill all the prisoners. Montjoy admits defeat and asks permission to bury the French dead. Henry places Williams's glove in Fluellen's cap.

4.8 Henry's joke works: Williams challenges Fluellen and is rewarded for his honesty. Casualties are reported: ten thousand French killed, twenty-nine English. The English army sings hymns to thank God for victory.

Act 5

Prologue The Chorus marks the passage of time and we are told of Henry's triumphant entry into London and his eventual return to France.

5.1 Fluellen forces Pistol to eat a leek for being disrespectful to an ancient Welsh tradition.

5.2 The French and English meet to agree a treaty. Henry proposes to Katherine and is accepted. The French king agrees to all the terms and hopes the royal marriage will unite the two nations in peace.

Epilogue The Chorus apologizes once again for the limited resources for such a weighty theme. He ends by explaining how all Henry's gains were lost in the reign of his son Henry VI.

Shakespeare uses a number of devices to keep his audience involved, such as:
- spectacular scenes
- comic scenes
- 'touching' scenes
- intimate scenes
- battle scenes
- scenes of political intrigue
- a love scene.

 Discuss... the story

With a partner look at the plot summaries and try to label each scene with one of the categories above. When you have made your list discuss how the variety of scenes keeps the play interesting. For each scene you should also think about:
- whether it advances the plot
- whether it advances our understanding of character
- whether it contrasts with the scenes or characters before or after it, and if so, why
- what dramatic impact the scene has.

Write about and role-play... **submitting the script**

1. Imagine you are William Shakespeare and that you have an idea for a play about Henry V. You want to persuade the other members of your acting company that your play is worth putting on. In groups of four, think about and make notes on what you consider makes your play better than any other about Henry V. Think about:
   - The audience: will it appeal to everyone?
   - The staging: how easy will it be to stage?
   - Dramatic impact: is it exciting and/or comic?
2. Now set up a role-play in which one member of the group presents the argument to the rest of the class who will take the role of Shakespeare's fellow actors.

  ### Discuss and write about... **a school production**

1. You are putting on a school production of *Henry V* and you want to shorten the running time.
   - Which scenes or parts of scenes could be left out?
   - Would it make any difference if the death of Falstaff were omitted?
   - Would you cut the discussion of the Salic law? Or do you think it is necessary for an understanding of Henry's motivation?
2. After your discussion, write a brief statement listing the cuts you have made and why you have made them.

2.3
1.2

  ### Design... **a poster**

Design a poster for *Henry V*, choosing as your main illustration what you think is the most interesting scene in the play.

Characters

Henry

Henry as Prince Hal

Shakespeare wrote two plays about Henry IV and it is in these that the future Henry V – or Prince Hal, as he was then known – is first introduced. He is, however, a very different character to the one we meet in *Henry V*: he lives an irresponsible life, mixing with thieves and drunkards, including Pistol, Bardolph and the likeable rogue Sir John Falstaff.

Even before the entrance of the king in *Henry V* we get a striking double-portrait of him from Canterbury, in which the riotous, fun-loving Prince Hal is contrasted with the learned, devout king that he became: **1.1** ▷

> CANTERBURY   Since his addiction was to courses vain,
> His companies <u>unletter'd</u>, rude, and shallow,   *uneducated*
> His hours fill'd up with riots, banquets, sports;
> And never noted in him any study.

But after his father's death:

> CANTERBURY   Never was such a sudden scholar made…
> Nor never <u>Hydra</u>-headed wilfulness   *a mythical monster with nine heads*
> So soon did lose his seat, and all at once,
> As in this king.

 ### Discuss… *Henry as Prince Hal*

You will find other references to Henry as a prince in Act 1 scene 2, Act 2 scene 1 and Act 2 scene 4.

1. What are we told of his character as prince?
2. Was his lifestyle appropriate for a future king?

Henry the diplomat

The play presents Henry's decision to invade France very carefully. Henry is cautious about entering into such a war and seeks advice from the Archbishop of Canterbury on his legal and moral rights to the crown of **1.2** ▷

France. Before Canterbury's very long discussion of the legal position in Act 1 scene 2 Henry warns him:

HENRY	For God doth know how many, now in health,	
	Shall drop their blood <u>in approbation</u>	*proving*
	Of what your reverence shall <u>incite</u> us to.	*urge*
	Therefore take heed how you <u>impawn our person</u>,	*commit me*
	How you awake our sleeping sword of war—	*to this*
	We charge you, in the name of God, take heed.	*enterprise*

After the archbishop has spoken Henry responds with the single, and therefore striking, line: 'May I with right and conscience make this claim?'

 Discuss... Henry's caution

1.2

❶ Why do you think Henry seeks advice from the Archbishop of Canterbury? Think about both religious and political reasons.
❷ What does Henry's caution and awareness of the consequences of his actions tell us about him as a king?
❸ How does this scene affect how we view the war with France?

1.2 At the end of Act 1 scene 2 the Dauphin sends Henry an insulting message and a present of tennis balls. In his reply Henry is angry, but cool and controlled. Look at the following lines from his speech:
● 'Tell him he hath made a match with such a wrangler/ That all the courts of France shall be disturbed/ with chases' [chases = points won in tennis; wrangler = a stubborn opponent]
● 'And we understand him well,/ How he comes o'er us with our wilder days,/ Not measuring what use we made of them.'
● 'And tell the pleasant Prince this mock of his/ Hath turn'd his balls to gun-stones...'

 Discuss... Henry's reply to the Dauphin

1.2

❶ How does Henry turn the Dauphin's joke of tennis balls into a threat?
❷ In the second quotation Henry is responding to the Dauphin's references to his wild youth. What do you think Henry is saying here? What does it tell us about him?
❸ Do we respect Henry at this point in the play?
❹ What does this incident tell us about the Dauphin and his understanding of Henry?
❺ What effect would the Dauphin's message have had on an Elizabethan audience?

Henry (Michael Sheen, right) receives the Dauphin's gift of tennis balls

 ## Act out... *Henry's reply to the Dauphin*   `1.2`

In pairs think about how Henry would be feeling and what his expression would be throughout this speech. Would he start sarcastically and become more menacing? Practise the speech together.

 ## Write... *a diary entry*

`1.2`

Imagine you are one of the noblemen who was present at this exchange between the king and the Dauphin's messenger. Write your diary entry for that day, detailing how the king handled the challenge and what you think of him and the Dauphin.

Henry the leader

We saw in Act 1 that Henry was unwilling to go to war unless his cause was just. Having been persuaded that it was, he assumes the role of leader of his army. But what kind of leader was he?

In Act 4 scene 1 Henry announces the belief that men will endure troubles   `4.1`
if they see their leaders suffering too: ''Tis good for men to love their present pains/ Upon example'. For this reason Henry is always at the forefront of the fighting, encouraging and inspiring his men. Look at the extract from Act 3 scene 1 (Henry's speech before Harfleur) on pages 41–42   `p41`
and the quotation below, which is part of Henry's speech before Agincourt:

HENRY	We few, we happy few, we band of brothers;		`4.3`
	For he to-day that sheds his blood with me	*shall be raised*
	Shall be my brother; be he ne'er so vile,	*to the rank of*
	This day <u>shall gentle his condition;</u>	*gentleman*

And gentlemen in England now-a-bed
Shall think themselves accurs'd they were not here,
And hold their manhoods cheap whiles any speaks
That fought with us upon Saint Crispin's day.

3.1
4.3

  *Discuss and write about... **Henry's leadership***

Discuss and make notes on the following points:
1. Who is Henry addressing, and what is the purpose of each speech?
2. What does he refer to in both speeches to inspire his men and make them feel proud?
3. In the extract above why are the few 'happy'? How does warfare make men 'brothers'? Why will men not involved in the battle envy the soldiers?
4. Do you think Henry was successful in achieving his purpose in these speeches?

 *Write... **a letter home***

Imagine you are a soldier in Henry's army. Write a letter home, telling your family what conditions were like in France, what the king said in his speeches at Harfleur and Agincourt and what you are feeling now about the campaign.

Henry the religious king

Throughout the play Henry is presented as a king with a strong religious faith, who believed that the outcome of the war with France lay 'within the will of God'. Before the battle of Agincourt he prays: 'O God of battles, steel my soldiers' hearts,/ Possess them not with fear!', and when, against all the odds, his army is successful, he refuses to take credit for the victory, but declares that 'God fought for us' and orders hymns in praise of God to be sung. The Chorus emphasizes Henry's piety in 'Being free from vainness and self-glorious pride' after Agincourt, and in giving all the honour to God.

1.2
4.1
4.8
5.Pr

Discuss... Henry as a religious king

1. Why do you think it was important to an Elizabethan audience that Henry was shown to be a religious king?
2. Do you think this has relevance for a modern audience?

Discuss... Henry's prayer

4.1

Read Henry's prayer at the end of Act 4 scene 1 ('O God of battles...').
Henry acknowledges his father's fault in usurping the throne. What has he done to seek forgiveness?

Henry the just king

Henry has to act as a judge on several occasions in the play; he tries and punishes both noble and common criminals. In Act 2 scene 2 he is called upon first to judge a common soldier. Here he is inclined to be forgiving of someone who has insulted him:

2.2

HENRY	<u>Enlarge</u> the man committed yesterday	*set free*
	That <u>rail'd</u> against our person. We consider	*shouted abuse*
	It was excess of wine that set him on;	
	And <u>on his more advice</u> we pardon him.	*now he's thought better of it*

The traitors Scroop, Cambridge and Grey are present during this scene and they urge Henry to be less merciful. As Scroop says: 'Let him be punish'd, sovereign, lest example/ Breed, by his sufferance, more of such a kind.' When their own treachery is revealed, their lack of mercy backfires on them. Read the following quotes from Henry's speech:

- 'The mercy that was quick in us but late/ By your own counsel is suppress'd and kill'd.'
- 'But, O,/ What shall I say to thee, Lord Scroop, thou cruel,/ Ingrateful, savage, and inhuman creature?/ Thou that didst bear the key of all my counsels,/ That knew'st the very bottom of my soul...'
- 'I will weep for thee;/ For this revolt of thine, methinks, is like/ Another fall of man.'
- 'Touching our person seek we no revenge;/ But we our kingdom's safety must so tender...'

*Discuss... **Henry's justice***

① What does Scroop's comment on how the soldier should be punished reveal about him?

② Look at the second and third quotations. What do they tell us about Henry's feelings towards the traitors? Do you think there is a conflict between his feelings as a man and as a king?

③ Do you think Henry's treatment of the soldier and the traitors was just and fair?

 *Write... **your last diary entry***

You are the traitor Scroop, sent to the Tower for treason and due to be executed tomorrow at dawn. Write your last diary entry.

Law and order are important to Henry even when he is at war. In Act 3 scene 6 Henry allows one of his own soldiers, Bardolph, to be condemned to death for stealing French property. Then he says:

HENRY   And we give express charge that in our marches through the country there be nothing compell'd from the villages, nothing taken but paid for, none of the French upbraided or abused in disdainful language; for when <u>lenity</u> and cruelty <u>play</u> for a kingdom the gentler gamester is the soonest winner.

gentleness
compete

 *Discuss and write about... **Bardolph's hanging***

In Henry's 'wilder days' Bardolph was one of his drinking companions. For stealing from a church, Bardolph is hanged on the orders of Essex, with the king's approval.

① Discuss whether you think Henry was just. Should he have spared his old friend?

② Write down his thoughts as he might have expressed them in his war journal that night. Think about the conflict he might have felt between his role as king and his feelings as a man.

Henry the common man and the king

Although he is king, Henry is also shown to be very much a human being with human frailties. The conflict between Henry's duty as king and his feelings as a man have been touched upon in the previous section. Henry himself refers directly to them in Act 4 scene 1 when in disguise he mixes with the men on the night before Agincourt. He confesses to Bates, Court and Williams that a king is essentially as ordinary as the next man:

HENRY   For though I speak it to you, I think the King is but a
man as I am: the violet smells to him as it doth to me;
the <u>element shows</u> to him as it doth to me; all his   *sky appears*
senses have but human conditions; his ceremonies
laid by, in his nakedness he appears but a man; and
though his <u>affections</u> are higher mounted than ours,   *emotions*
yet, <u>when they stoop, they stoop with the like wing</u>.   *they have the same*
                                                              effect on him

4.1 ▷

Yet Henry's responsibilities as a king have to come before his personal feelings. Although he has fears, like the common soldier, he cannot show them in case he disheartens his army. In his long soliloquy on 'ceremony' (a **soliloquy** is a speech in which a character speaks their thoughts either to him/herself or directly to the audience), he shows what responsibilities and burdens a king must bear that the average man is free of:

HENRY   What infinite heart's ease
Must kings neglect that private men enjoy!
And what have kings that privates have not too,
Save ceremony—save general ceremony?

4.1 ▷

But what is it to be a king? What is the value of ceremony? Henry answers himself: 'What drink'st thou oft, instead of homage sweet,/ But poison'd flattery?' The king cannot sleep as soundly as the wretched slave; and he must ever be on guard to preserve peace so that his subjects may enjoy it.

 ## Discuss... *being a king*

1. Do you feel sympathy for Henry?
2. Would you like to be a king?
3. Would you be as concerned about your subjects as he is?

23

Write... *a royal agony letter*

There were so many kings around in the Middle Ages that it is possible to imagine they had their own magazine. Choose an incident from the play in which Henry is faced with a difficult decision and write a letter asking for advice from *King!* magazine.

Henry the joker

In Act 4 scene 1 Williams says that he doesn't believe the king's claim not to allow himself to be ransomed. The disguised Henry is offended and challenges Williams to settle the disagreement after the battle. They agree to swap gloves and wear them in their 'bonnets' after the battle so that they will recognize each other. But later, Henry gives the glove to Fluellen as a practical joke. Read this section of Act 4 scene 1 and the sequel in Act 4 scene 8.

 ## Discuss... *Henry the joker*

1. Do you like playing practical jokes?
2. How do you feel about people who won't unbend and have a joke?
3. Why do you think Shakespeare shows this side of Henry's character?
4. Why does he show it immediately after the battle?

 ## Role-play... *the incident of the glove*

Role-play the characters of Williams, King Henry and Fluellen, allowing each to tell his side of the story as if they were having a friendly drink together afterwards.

Henry the lover

Kenneth Branagh as Henry and Emma Thompson as Katherine in the 1989 film version of Henry V

5.2 >

Our final encounter with Henry, in Act 5 scene 2, shows him in all his power at the French court, yet in the middle of the scene he is portrayed as an awkward lover:

HENRY Marry, if you would put me to verses or to dance for your sake, Kate, why you undid me; for the one I have neither words nor <u>measure</u>, and for the other I have no strength in <u>measure</u>, yet a reasonable <u>measure</u> in strength. If I could win a lady at leap-frog, or by vaulting into my saddle with my armour on my back, under the correction of bragging be it spoken, I should quickly leap into wife.

measure = 1 rhythm, 2 dancing, 3 amount

---

 *Discuss... **Henry the lover***

1. Do you accept Henry's claim to be a man of action not words?
2. What sort of words is he more comfortable with?
3. Why do you think Shakespeare has shown Henry to be vulnerable as a lover? After all, Katherine had no choice in whom she married.

Henry's darker side

 *Discuss... **Henry's darker side***

Are all of Henry's actions positive? As a class, discuss the following areas:

1. What about the way he lets the traitor lords condemn themselves in Act 2 scene 1? Is he playing with them? 2.1 >
2. Is he serious in Act 3 scene 3 when he says he can barely control his soldiers? 3.3 >
3. Why doesn't he comment on Bardolph's death in Act 3 scene 6? 3.6 >
4. Could his treatment of Williams and Fluellen in Act 4 be considered a cruel abuse of his own power?
5. Henry makes some very long speeches. Is he too fond of the sound of his own voice?

 *Write... **your own view***

During the discussion on Henry's 'darker side' you must have disagreed with another member of the class on certain points. Write a letter to this person, explaining why you disagree with them. Post your letters in a classroom mailbox for delivery the next day.

Hot seat... *Henry*

One student, who knows the role well, should take the part of Henry. The rest of the class should prepare questions based on incidents in the play which show the positive and negative sides of the king. Interview Henry about his role and whether he enjoys it.

Other views of Henry

When studying any character you also need to consider the views of other characters. As you might expect, these views differ: the Dauphin will not have the same attitude to Henry as, say, Captain Fluellen or the Duke of Exeter. In deciding whether to believe a statement about Henry by another character, first think about what is likely to influence that character's views, then look at Henry's actions and decide whether they support the character's views.

Write about... *assessing Henry*

Copy out the comments (below) that have been made about Henry by different characters. Write down in each case:

1. whether you think the comment is trustworthy, using your knowledge of the character who made it
2. whether you agree or disagree with it, using evidence from your knowledge of Henry to support your view.

1.1
1.1
2.1
2.2
2.4
3.7

- 'The King is full of grace and fair regard' (Archbishop of Canterbury, Act 1 scene 1).
- 'a true lover of the holy Church' (Bishop of Ely, Act 1 scene 1)
- 'The King hath run bad humours on the knight' (Nym, Act 2 scene 1)
- 'Never was monarch better fear'd and lov'd than is your Majesty' (Cambridge, Act 2 scene 2)
- 'a vain, giddy, shallow, humorous youth' (Dauphin, Act 2 scene 4)
- 'a wretched and peevish fellow is this King of England' (Duke of Orleans, Act 3 scene 7)

Your response to the first comment may look something like this:

> 'The King is full of grace and fair regard' (Archbishop of Canterbury, 1.1). We can't completely trust this comment: Canterbury has his own reasons to be flattering about the king – he hopes to persuade the king to go to war to distract him from taxing the Church. However, the king does show grace and fair regard in listening to Canterbury's advice in Act 1 scene 2.

Role-play... *the different Henrys*

We have seen Henry as diplomat, king, common man, leader and lover – a many-sided character. Working in groups, present the roles of Henry separately, beginning '*I am the Henry who...*'. The last Henry is the complete man, uniting all the different sides.

A range of characters

We have studied Henry's character in detail – now let us look at some of the other characters. They fall into several groups:

- **Royalty:** for example, the Dauphin, Katherine, King Charles of France
- **Nobles:** for example, Exeter, Constable of France
- **Churchmen:** for example, the Archbishop of Canterbury
- **Officers:** for example, Fluellen, Gower, Jamy, Macmorris
- **Soldiers and others:** for example, Williams, Pistol, Bardolph, Boy

Within these groups there are several nationalities: English, Welsh, Scots, Irish and French. Shakespeare presents a wide spectrum, from the highest to the humblest, some with distinctive personalities.

 ## Write... *a character study*

To help you understand the other characters you need to think about their actions throughout the play.

1. Choose a character from the play and use the plot summary on pages 13–15 to find out which scenes the character appears in.
2. Then read the scenes carefully. Using a table like the one below, make brief notes on the character's actions and what this tells us about them and their role in the plot.

3.2

	Fluellen	
Act and scene	**Action**	**What this shows**
Act 3 scene 2	He drives Bardolph, Nym and Pistol back to the fighting.	He dislikes cowards.
	He becomes involved in a dispute with the captains about the 'disciplines of war'.	He likes theorizing and has strong views on conducting a war. He appears comical when he tries to discuss this in the middle of a battle.

3. When you have completed your notes write a detailed portrait of your character.

Themes

War

You will not be surprised to know that the word 'war' occurs ninety-nine times in *Henry V*. The play presents us with a sweeping vision of war, revealing it in all its moods from glory to suffering.

Honour and glory

Throughout the play the Chorus paints a positive image of war in which honour, courage and loyalty play a great part. At the beginning of Act 2, for example, the Chorus tell us:

2.Pr

> **CHORUS** Now all the youth of England are on fire...
> and honour's thought
> Reigns solely in the breast of every man.

3.1
p41
4.3

Henry's speeches to his soldiers also draw on the positive side of war: his speech at Harfleur in Act 3 scene 1 arouses feelings of honour and defiant bravery (see pages 41–42). Henry's speech in Act 4 scene 3 emphasizes the pride that his soldiers will have in their victory.

The dark side of war

The actions of the play also reveal the less honorable and glorious side of war, in which cowardice, lawlessness and greed have the upper hand.

 ### Discuss... *the dark side of war*

2.1
3.2
3.6

Look at and consider the following:
1. Bardolph, Nym and Pistol's reasons for going to war.
2. The Boy's speech in Act 3 scene 2 (beginning 'As young as I am').
3. Bardolph's theft of the 'pax' (picture) (Act 3 scene 6).

Do you think that Shakespeare included these scenes to criticize war, to provide a background for the bravery and heroism or simply to be realistic?

3.1

The play also presents the gory reality of war. Henry's speech to the governor of Harfleur grimly details the grisly outcome of not surrendering.

The dire effects of war on ordinary people are emphasized by Essex in Act 2 scene 4 and by Williams in his debate with Henry in Act 4 scene 1:

2.4 >

WILLIAMS But if the cause be not good, the King himself hath a heavy reckoning to make when all those legs and arms and heads, chopp'd off in a battle, shall join together at the <u>latter day</u> and cry all 'We died at such a place'—some swearing, some crying for a surgeon, some upon their wives left poor behind them, some upon the debts they owe, some upon their children rawly left. I am afeard there are few die well that die in a battle; for how can they charitably dispose of anything when blood is their argument?

Day of Judgement

4.1 >

Kenneth Branagh and Brian Blessed, 1989

  Discuss and write about... death in battle

4.1
4.6 >

In pairs, look carefully at Williams' speech above, and compare it with Exeter's description of the heroic deaths of Suffolk and York in Act 4 scene 6.
1. Why is one in prose and the other in verse?
2. Which speech do you find more realistic?
3. How was Shakespeare's audience meant to respond to these two speeches? Is the modern response different? Is one wrong and the other right, or do they both tell us something about death in battle?
4. Is it possible to decide what Shakespeare himself thought about war, or does he simply stand back and show every side?
Write a brief summary of your feelings.

Design... *a poster*

First make a selection of quotations which illustrate the contrasting images of war in the play. Then use your quotations as part of the design of a poster for the play. The poster should express a definite attitude to war, either for or against.

Kingship

Elizabethans believed in the divine right of kings, according to which kings were given their right to rule directly from God (see page 8). *Henry V* would therefore have been especially interesting to an Elizabethan audience, as it considers the responsibilities and virtues of the ideal king.

A good ruler...
- is pious (religious)
- listens to advice
- administers justice fairly to people of all social classes
- leads by example
- is successful in war
- cares for ordinary people
- has a sense of humour.

 Write about... *kingship*

Look at the following quotations from the play. Write down the list of qualities of a good ruler (above) and next to each quality write the quotation you think matches it.

1. 'We are no tyrant, but a Christian king'
2. 'May I with right and conscience make this claim?'
3. 'Enlarge the man committed yesterday/ Who rail'd against our person'
4. 'We would not die in that man's company/ That fears his fellowship to die with us'
5. 'The day is yours'
6. 'And we give express charge that in our marches through the country there be nothing compell'd from the villages, nothing taken but paid for'
7. 'In loving me you should love the friend of France; for I love France so well that I would not part with a village of it; I will have it all mine.'

 Discuss... *Henry's kingship*

In pairs, discuss the evidence you have collected in the Characters section of Henry's kingship. Is Shakespeare's Henry V meant to be a portrait of an ideal king?

The disadvantages of being a king are also explored in the play, especially in Act 4 scene 1. See the Character section (page 23).

4.1
p23

Patriotism and unity

Henry V can be seen as a great patriotic play. Shakespeare was writing at a time when Queen Elizabeth had raised the nation's pride to new heights. The themes of national identity and unity in the play would have received an approving response from the audience.

One of the most popular film productions of the play was made by Laurence Olivier in 1944, when the Allies were again invading France in the Second World War.

The Chorus plays an important part in stirring patriotic feelings.

 Write about… the Chorus' attitude to war

2.Pr
3.Pr
4.Pr

In pairs look at how the Chorus conveys patriotism in the prologues to Acts 2, 3 and 4. Jot down notes under the following headings:
- How are the preparations for war described?
- What kind of images of Henry and his army does the Chorus use in Acts 2 and 3?
- How is the prologue to Act 4 different?
- What use does the Chorus make of classical references?
- How does the Chorus portray the French?

*Discuss... **national pride***

There are, of course, successes and achievements other than military victory that make a country feel proud of itself – achievements in sport or science, for instance. Open up a discussion on what brings out national pride in a country.

The English v. the French

The French too have their national pride and feel great shame at their defeat; but coming after their vain boasting and sarcastic ridicule of the English, it almost seems deserved. The ending of the play, however, brings a peace that, for the time being, unites the two countries in what the French king calls 'Christian-like accord'.

 5.2

 *Write about... **the two sides***

① Look at the table below. On the left are various features of the English army, showing its character, behaviour and attitude. Fill in the right-hand column to help you compare the same features in the French army.

② When you have completed the table, decide why Shakespeare created such a contrast between the two sides.

English	French
The army contains several nationalities	
It contains men of all ranks	
The nobles are united and dedicated to Henry	
The army is small and weakened by sickness	
It is operating in a foreign country and must live off the land	
The king calls them brothers, friends and countrymen	
Their losses at Agincourt are 29 dead	

Shakespeare's way with words

Shakespeare's plays have remained popular for four hundred years. This is partly because they contain great drama and partly because of the language, particularly the imagery, which makes the speeches imaginative and memorable.

Imagery

Powerful imagery can be created by the appropriate choice of words, but it is often extended by the use of figurative language. This occurs when a comparison is made between the thing being described and an image or verbal picture that illustrates it. The most common forms of this imagery are:

- **Simile**, when a comparison is made using 'like' or 'as': 'His nose was as sharp as a pen'. `2.3 >`
- **Metaphor**, when 'like' or 'as' are omitted and one thing is said to *be* another: 'a good heart, Kate, is the sun and the moon'. `5.2 >`
- **Personification**, when an idea or object is described as though it were a person: 'Fortune is Bardolph's foe, and frowns on him'. `3.6 >`

Analogies are also used to express ideas. An analogy is a detailed comparison of two situations, one of which is used to comment on the other. There are two in *Henry V*. The first is Canterbury's comparison of the people of England to bees working together for a common aim (Act 1 scene 2); the second is Burgundy's comparison of a neglected garden to the state of France (Act 5 scene 1). `1.2 >` `5.1 >`

Write about... *figurative language*

Copy these quotations into your books and for each one identify the figure of speech being used: simile, metaphor or personification:

1.2
① **WESTMORELAND** For once the eagle England being in prey,
To her unguarded nest the weasel Scot
Comes sneaking, and so sucks her princely eggs,
Playing the mouse in the absence of the cat,
To tear and havoc more than she can eat.

1.2
② **HENRY** ... the Scot on his unfurnish'd kingdom
Came pouring, like the tide into a breach

4.1
③ **HENRY** And what art thou, thou idol Ceremony?
What kind of god art thou, that suffer'st more
Of mortal griefs than do thy worshippers?

Prose and verse

Most of *Henry V* is written in **blank verse**, which is unrhymed but contains ten syllables and five stresses in each line. The end of a scene is often signalled by a 'couplet' when two of these lines are rhymed. Blank verse is usually used for serious (or 'high') characters, but in this play even Pistol speaks in blank verse at times.

4.3
 ## Perform... *blank verse*

Look at Henry's speech before Agincourt in Act 4 scene 3. Read it aloud twice: first ignoring the line endings, then giving full weight to the rhythm of the verse. Which version is better?

Prose is 'ordinary' writing, without any set rhythm or formal rules. There are no particular stresses and definitely no rhymes. Shakespeare tended to use prose for his comic (or 'low') characters, but there were no strict rules. Occasionally the speeches of 'high' characters are also in prose.

 ## Discuss... *prose scenes*

2.1
① Look at the argument between Pistol and Nym at the beginning of Act 2 scene 1. Why would formal blank verse have been inappropriate here? Why are some of the speeches in blank verse?

4.1
5.2
② Why did Shakespeare decide to write these scenes in prose: a) the night scene before Agincourt; b) the proposal scene with Katherine?

The language of expression

By a careful choice of words and images Shakespeare can emphasize a
character's thoughts and feelings. Look at the passage below as an
illustration of this 'way with words':

CONSTABLE To horse, you gallant Princes! straight to horse! `4.2`
         Do but behold yon poor and starved band,
         And your fair show shall suck away their souls,
         Leaving them but the <u>shales</u> and husks of men. *shells*
         There is not work enough for all our hands;
         Scarce blood enough in all their sickly veins
         To give each naked <u>curtle-axe</u> a stain *cutlass*
         That our French gallants shall to-day draw out,
         And sheathe for lack of sport. Let us but blow on them,
         The vapour of our valour will o'erturn them.

Write about... *the language of expression*

1 Look at Constable's speech above. `4.2`
- Which expressions emphasize the superiority of the French?
- Which expressions emphasize the poor state of the English army?
- What attitude is behind Constable's words?
- To make his point, Constable is exaggerating. Can you find some examples?
- Certain words are linked. For instance, for the French: 'gallant... fair... gallants... valour'. For the English: 'poor... starved...' Can you continue the list?

2 You can use this method to look at Shakespeare's language in other speeches. In Montjoy's description of the battlefield, for example (Act 4 scene 7): `4.7`
- Which words emphasize the bloodshed?
- Which words contrast the ordinary soldiers with the nobles?
- Why does Montjoy address Henry twice as 'great King'?

Rhetoric

You have probably noticed that there are some very long speeches in
Henry V! For a modern audience this might seem to be a weakness in the
play, but Shakespeare and his audience actually enjoyed well-constructed,
elaborate speeches. In fact, the art of making speeches to persuade an
audience was studied in schools and universities and was called **rhetoric**.
Getting a point across is just as important in public life today, in our age

of mass media, public relations experts and spin doctors. If you listen to a great political speech you will hear the same tones, and techniques as Henry used in the play.

www.libdems.o

Henry (Kenneth Branagh) delivering a rousing speech

A modern politician

If we look at certain speeches in the play we can identify some of the techniques used in speech-making and ask how effective they are in getting the listeners' attention and persuading them of the argument.

First refer to Henry's speech before Harfleur (pages 41–42). You will see that Shakespeare has used many of the literary techniques we studied above: simile, metaphor and personification. To these we can add:

- **Apostrophe**, when the speaker addresses his audience directly: 'Once more unto the breach, dear friends'.
- **Alliteration**, the repetition of a sound at the beginning of words: 'Stiffen the sinews, summon up the blood'.
- **Repetition**, when a word or phrase is repeated for emotional emphasis: 'On, on, you noblest English'.

3.1

 *Study... **Henry's speech before Harfleur***

1. Write down all the words referring to the body, starting with 'ears'.
2. Find the similes. Are they well chosen?
3. Alliteration gives rhythm and emphasis. Quote some examples.
4. Quote some examples of repetition.
5. What makes the last line an effective climax to the speech?
6. Remind yourself of the work you did on this speech in the Characters section (page 20). Do you think these rhetorical techniques reinforce the purpose and meaning of the speech?

Shakespeare's dramatic skill

Shakespeare had already written seven plays about this period of English history by the time he came to *Henry V*. He knew how to present historical events and he knew how to keep his audience entertained. In the section on Plot (see page 15) we saw how he used a variety of scenes to change the pace and tone of his story. He also included a wide range of characters. However, he still had a few more tricks up his sleeve.

Dramatic irony

Dramatic irony is when the audience knows more about the action than the characters do themselves. Look again at Act 4 scene 1, in which Henry visits his camp in disguise on the eve of the battle of Agincourt. In this scene Shakespeare makes use of dramatic irony: *we* know that the soldiers are talking to the king, but *they* do not. Many of the words of both the soldiers and the king play on this irony, such as when Bates says 'I would he were here alone'. The irony is continued in later scenes with the incident of Williams's glove; there it adds to the comedy of the play.

In Act 2 scene 2 the audience knows that the plot against Henry has been discovered but the conspirators don't. There's dramatic irony in their flattering speeches and particularly in Scroop's insistence that the man who offended the king should be punished!

Occasionally, looking back, we can see that a situation or a speech has been ironical. In Act 4 scene 2, for example, the French boast about their superiority and Constable says: 'A very little little let us do/ And all is done.' He is thinking of victory – but his words are equally true of the French defeat.

 Discuss... *dramatic irony*

4.1

1. How does Shakespeare's use of dramatic irony in Act 4 scene 1 affect your reaction to Henry's conversation with his soldiers? What effect does it have on the way the plot develops?

2.2

2. Look at the early part of the 'traitor' scene (Act 2 scene 2) and discuss how your knowledge of Cambridge, Scroop and Gray's treachery affects your reaction to what they say.

Comedy

For a serious history play there is a fair amount of comedy in *Henry V*. This is provided by characters such as Pistol, Nym, Bardolph and Fluellen, as well as by comic situations such as the joke Henry plays on Williams.

We can identify some of the more obvious comic scenes as:

2.1 • The argument between Nym and Pistol
3.2 • The dispute between Fluellen, Macmorris, Jamy and Gower
4.4 • Pistol and his French captive
4.8 • The argument between Williams and Fluellen
5.1 • Fluellen making Pistol eat a leek.

 Discuss... *the use of comic scenes in the plot*

p13

1. Use the plot summaries (see pages 13–15) to remind yourself of these comic scenes. Discuss each one and decide why Shakespeare introduced it at that point in the play.
   • Why do you think Shakespeare has included these comic scenes in a play about war?
   • Are they completely separate from the main theme?
   • How would the play be different without them?

2. Choose one of the scenes and look at it carefully. Discuss what you think makes it comic. Think about the language, the action and how it would be performed on stage.

 Write... *notes for the actors*

Based on your discussion, write brief notes giving advice on making the scene funny. Your notes for the actors in Act 4 scene 4, for example, may begin like this: ▸▸

> The three actors are Pistol, the French soldier and the Boy. The comedy comes
> mainly from Pistol's character and from the fact that he can't understand
> French (nor can the audience, but that doesn't make the scene less amusing).
> When Pistol says 'Yield, cur!', he should make an exaggerated gesture with his
> sword.

4.4 >

- Your notes to Pistol might continue by telling him to look at the French words he repeats and misunderstands; his French pronunciation; his dramatic vocabulary; how he is threatening until he's offered money.
- Your notes to the French soldier might ask him to think about what actions and mannerisms would best bring out the humour of the situation.
- You might tell the Boy to play to the audience more, and to consider what change comes at the end of the scene.

 Perform... *a comic scene*

As a class share out the comic scenes (or parts of scenes) mentioned above
and rehearse them in groups. Perform each scene with the rest of the class
as audience.

The language of comedy

Another form of comedy in the play comes from the words that a character
uses. In the English language lesson that Alice gives to Princess Katherine
(Act 3 scene 4) the comedy is in the pronunciation and word-play.

3.4 >

 Discuss... *the comedy of the language lesson*

1. Can you quote some examples of word-play and comic pronunciation in this scene? Why has Shakespeare selected these particular words for Katherine to learn?
2. How could the actors playing Katherine and Alice make this scene funny? Think about gestures, facial expressions and pronunciation.
3. Do you think it matters that many people would not be able to understand the words in this scene? Is Shakespeare simply poking fun at funny foreigners here, or does he have a more serious point to make about the divisions between England and France?

Fluellen's English is another source of verbal comedy in the play because,
as Gower says, he can't speak English 'in the native garb'. He has a
peculiar and amusing style of speech, with his 'p's for 'b's, his 'look you's'
and his habit of never using one word when several will do.

5.1 >

Shakespeare has also given Pistol his own style of verbal comedy, full of
pompous poetry and alliteration:

4.4

FRENCH SOLDIER	Monsieur le Fer.
BOY	He says his name is Master Fer.
PISTOL	Master Fer! I'll fer him, and <u>firk</u> him, and <u>ferret</u> him—discuss the same in French unto him.

thrash

worry him as a ferret worries a rabbit

The Chorus

Henry V is Shakespeare's only history play that makes use of a chorus. He fulfils an important function in helping the audience follow the plot and in stressing the patriotic nature of the play. In the prologue to Act 4, for example, the Chorus uses many of the literary devices we saw in the Agincourt speech, but it is descriptive rather than persuasive.

4.Pr

The Chorus (Tony Britton) in an RSC production, 1994

4.Pr

  ### Act... the Chorus in Act 4

1. Before 'acting' the Chorus, study it as an example of Shakespeare's dramatic skill:
   - What does it aim to do in the theatre? (Think about the Elizabethan audience.)
   - What literary techniques are used to achieve this aim?
2. Instead of having one person read the speech, divide it up for several speakers. A second group should produce the sound effects.
   - Starting at 'the hum of either army', note down all the sounds that are mentioned and decide how to make them.
   - What atmosphere do you want to create? How can you produce it?

In the director's chair

The book you have been studying in class is not the play, *Henry V*, it is only the script. If you are really going to understand the play you need to think carefully about what would be happening on stage. The best way to do this is to appoint yourself director of a production.

The director of any play is in charge of all aspects of the production, from the costumes and lighting down to the way individual words should be pronounced. You will look at how to prepare two scenes from Act 3.

The first job is to understand what is happening in the scenes. Read the following extract in pairs. It consists of Act 3 scene 1 and the beginning of Act 3 scene 2. The English army is besieging the French town of Harfleur.

Scene 1. France. Before Harfleur
Alarum. Enter the King, Exeter, Bedford, Gloucester, and soldiers with scaling-ladders

3.1 ▷

HENRY Once more unto the <u>breach</u>, dear friends, once more;	*a break in the*
Or close the wall up with our English dead.	*town's defences*
In peace there's nothing so becomes a man	
As modest stillness and humility;	
But when the blast of war blows in our ears,	
Then imitate the action of the tiger:	
Stiffen the sinews, summon up the blood,	
Disguise fair nature with <u>hard-favour'd</u> rage;	*hard-faced*
Then lend the eye a terrible aspect;	
Let it pry through the <u>portage</u> of the head	*portholes*
Like the brass cannon: let the brow o'erwhelm it	
As fearfully as doth a <u>galled</u> rock	*eroded*
O'erhang and jutty his <u>confounded</u> base,	*damaged*
Swill'd with the wild and wasteful ocean.	
Now set the teeth and stretch the nostril wide;	
Hold hard the breath, and bend up every spirit	
To his full height. On, on, you noblest English,	
Whose blood is <u>fet from fathers of war-proof</u>—	*descended*
Fathers that like so many Alexanders	*from war-*
Have in these parts from morn till even fought,	*hardened*
And sheath'd their swords for lack of argument.	*fathers*
Dishonour not your mothers; now attest	
That those whom you call'd fathers did beget you.	

Be copy now to men of grosser blood,   *set an*
And teach them how to war. And you, good yeomen,   *example to*
Whose limbs were made in England, show us here   *lesser men*
The mettle of your pasture; let us swear
That you are worth your breeding—which I doubt not;
For there is none of you so mean and base
That hath not noble lustre in your eyes.
I see you stand like greyhounds in the slips,
Straining upon the start. The game's afoot:
Follow your spirit; and upon this charge
Cry 'God for Harry, England, and Saint George!'

Exeunt. Alarum, and <u>chambers</u> go off   *cannons*

Scene 2. Before Harfleur
Enter Nym, Bardolph, Pistol, and Boy

BARDOLPH   On, on, on, on, on! to the breach, to the breach!

NYM   Pray thee, Corporal, stay; <u>the knocks are too hot</u>, and   *the fighting is*
for mine own part I have not a case of lives. The   *too fierce*
humour of it is too hot; that is the very <u>plain-song</u> of it.   *simple truth*

PISTOL   The <u>plain-song</u> is most just; for humours do abound.   *simple melody*
Knocks go and come; God's vassals drop and die;
    And sword and shield
    In bloody field
    Doth win immortal fame.

BOY   Would I were in an alehouse in London! I would give
all my fame for a pot of ale and safety.

PISTOL   And I:
If wishes would prevail with me,
My purpose should not fail with me,
    But thither would I hie.

BOY   As duly, but not as <u>truly</u>,   *in tune*
     As bird doth sing on bough.

Enter Fluellen

FLUELLEN   Up to the breach, you dogs!
Avaunt, you cullions!

Driving them forward

PISTOL   Be merciful, great duke, to <u>men of mould</u>.   *men of clay*
Abate thy rage, abate thy manly rage;   *(mere humans)*

Abate thy rage, great duke.
Good bawcock, bate thy rage. Use lenity, sweet chuck.

NYM These be good <u>humours</u>. Your honour wins <u>bad humours</u>. | moods
                                                                      | bad tempers

Exeunt all but Boy

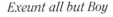

 Discuss... *the scenes*

3.1
3.2

❶ In groups discuss what is happening in these scenes and what events have led up to them.

❷ How does Henry try to build up the courage of his soldiers? What arguments does he use? (Use your notes on character on pages 19–20). **p19**

❸ What is the effect of Bardolph's speech after Henry's? What attitude is Bardolph expressing?

❹ Do you think the sudden change from heroic effort to mockery and near cowardice is effective?

❺ Why do you think Pistol and the Boy deliver their lines in 'plainsong'?

 Direct... *the scenes*

3.1
3.2

You should now think about putting the scenes on the stage. Here are some points to consider:

❶ Decide on the pace. Which parts would be slow? Which fast? The sentence structure might help you to decide this.

❷ How would you signal the change of mood and tempo after Henry's speech?

❸ What kind of stage are you using? Decide on stage layout, scenery, sound, lighting, props and costumes. Make a list of what you would need. Draw a diagram of the set. How will you suggest the besieged town and the battle that is going on?

❹ How would the actors be placed? How would they move? What gestures would they make?

❺ How do you interpret the scenes? Is Henry to appear 'over the top' or inspiring? Should we sympathize with the others or see them as cowardly and mean-spirited?

 Act... *the scenes*

3.1
3.2

❶ Rehearse the scenes in accordance with your decisions and interpretation, then perform them for the class.

❷ How did the interpretations differ? What does this tell us about the way Shakespeare can be presented in the theatre and on film?

Shakespeare and NCTs

Assessment Objectives

Your Shakespeare paper is part of your National Curriculum Tests. It is designed to test your ability to understand and respond to:

- Shakespeare's presentation of ideas
- The motivation and behaviour of characters
- The development of plot
- The language of the scenes
- The overall impact of the scenes
- The presentation of the scenes on stage.

You will also be assessed on the quality of your writing.

In the exam you will be asked a question on a scene which you have studied beforehand, but you will be expected to relate this scene to the play as a whole.

Probably the most important, and difficult, thing to remember in your exam is that you are writing about a play, not just words on a page. Some questions in the exam remind you of this, and ask for things like advice to actors, or your views if you were a director, but this very important fact should be at the back of your mind in any answer you attempt.

Shakespeare's presentation of ideas Shakespeare developed his ideas, or themes, through both the plot and the language of the play. But remember that he was writing for the theatre. In getting an idea across he would have had to consider how it would work on the stage.

The motivation and behaviour of characters The behaviour of characters – what they say and do – is relatively easy to see and to comment on. A character's motivation (why they behave as they do) can only be judged by assessing the character throughout the play. You can then relate their motivation to their actions in the scene you are writing about.

The development of plot You can only really understand the scene you have been given if you know how it fits into the action of the play as a whole. Is it:

- developing the plot
- a major crisis in the play itself
- building up tension
- raising a smile
- advancing our understanding of the characters?

The language of the scene You will have spent time before the exam looking at the language of the scene that has been set. Understanding the language, therefore, should not be a problem. What you need to discuss is the effect of the language on the characters in the scene and on the audience.

The overall impact of the scene To get the best marks you need to be able to discuss how your scene works on all its different levels, including how it might affect the audience.

The presentation of the scene on stage You need to be able to express ideas on how the script might be brought to life by real actors on a real stage.

REMEMBER You will also be assessed on the quality of your writing, so it is important to write clearly, using the correct vocabulary, spelling and punctuation.

How to do well in your Shakespeare paper

- Read the whole play at least once.
- Go and see a production of the play.
- Watch film versions of the play.
- Act out your set scene.
- Know your set scene really well. Make sure you know the meaning of all the words.
- Know how your scene fits into the play as a whole.
- Have a good idea of what Shakespeare is trying to do in your set scene.
- Practise writing under timed conditions.

Using quotations and evidence

When you are writing about a scene you need to provide evidence for the examiner. The best way of doing this is to refer closely to the text or to provide a quotation.

'Referring closely to the text' does not mean retelling what is happening in your chosen scene. You need to make a point about what you are saying. For instance, in the prologue to Act 1 you might wish to say something about the Chorus comparing the reality of sitting and watching a play with the reality of the events described. Your answer might look something like this:

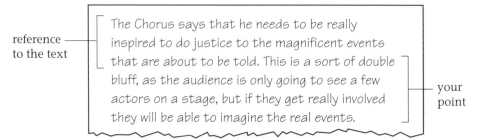

reference to the text — The Chorus says that he needs to be really inspired to do justice to the magnificent events that are about to be told. This is a sort of double bluff, as the audience is only going to see a few actors on a stage, but if they get really involved they will be able to imagine the real events. — your point

Short quotations are best used when you wish to show the exact words that have given you the idea for your answer. You place short quotations inside inverted commas and on the same line as the rest of your writing. For example:

Here the Chorus is making unflattering comparisons between the theatre, which he calls a 'cockpit' and a 'wooden O' to emphasize their — short quotations
smallness, and the huge scenes and events that are about to unfold.

Longer quotations are used when you want to comment on whole lines of the play or a piece of dialogue. You lay them out exactly as you find them in the play, but if there is only one person speaking it is not necessary to give their name.

Sample questions

Examples of the kind of questions you will meet in your Shakespeare paper follow on pages 47–48. They all relate to *Henry V*.

Act 2 scene 2

TASK 1

In this scene Henry exposes the treachery of the lords Scroop, Cambridge and Grey.

Comment in detail on the way that Henry handles this situation and what it shows us about his character.

Before you begin to write you should think about:
- the purpose of Bedford, Westmoreland and Exeter's conversation before the traitors appear;
- what the speeches by the three lords demonstrate, before their treachery is revealed;
- how Henry responds as a man and as a king;
- why Henry begins and ends his part in the scene talking about the expedition to France;
- the language used throughout the scene.

Read the task again before you write your answer.

Before writing your answer to Task 1, you should make notes based on the guidance given in the bullet points. As you look through the scene you should select quotations to back up your views. Your notes might look like this:

- General introduction – Henry is on his way to France and is setting his house in order before he goes. This includes dealing with drunken soldiers as well as traitors. Scene shows Henry as man and king.
- Exeter, Westmoreland and Bedford set the scene and prepare the audience for what is to come. They underline the depth of the treachery (by 'the man that was his bedfellow') and the efficiency of Henry in finding it out.
- Cambridge, Scroop and Grey are given the chance to show how devious they are in their comments both on the expedition and on the drunken soldier. By urging that no mercy should be shown to the soldier they are condemning themselves – the audience is aware of this.
- Henry's long speech is a personal response to the situation. He is particularly hurt by Scroop's treachery as he thought they were friends. He says he will 'weep' for the traitors because of the depth of their sin, but as king he has no hesitation in condemning them to death.
- This part of the play emphasizes Henry's decisiveness. He is on his way to France and nothing, not even betrayal by his friends, will stop him. The audience is also eager to get on to the battle scenes.
- The scene uses formal court language. The traitors behave as if on trial and confess their faults in the hope of gaining mercy. Henry uses strong imagery to describe the depth of the treachery.

Write... answers to sample questions

Look at Tasks 2 and 3 below. Write your answers to these tasks in note form, in a similar way to the notes on page 47. Choose one of the three tasks and write your notes up for homework. Remember to write clearly, using the correct vocabulary, spelling and punctuation.

4.3

Act 4 scene 3

TASK 2

In this scene Henry inspires his men as they prepare for the battle of Agincourt. He makes a stirring speech and rejects a chance to surrender.

Imagine you are a soldier in King Henry's army. Write about how the way Henry spoke and acted affected you.

Before you begin to write you should decide how a soldier might feel about:
- whether there were enough soldiers to fight;
- whether the king valued your services;
- what the king thought of your side's chances in the battle;
- some of the memorable and striking things that Henry said;
- what you thought of his rejection of the French offer.

Read the task again before you write your answer.

5.2

Act 5 scene 2 from the exit of the French King to his re-entry

TASK 3

In this part of the scene Henry and Katherine are left alone so that Henry can propose to the princess.

Imagine you are going to direct this scene for your year group. Explain how you would want Henry and Katherine to act in this part of the scene and how you would bring out their developing relationship.

Before you begin to write you should think about these questions:
- What would you say to the student playing Henry about his approach to Katherine? Is he to act nervous? confident? confused?
- What would you tell the student playing Katherine about her attitude to Henry? Is she to act suspicious? cautious? secretly pleased?
- What role should Alice play – stern chaperone or delighted onlooker?
- How would you deal with the French-speaking in the scene?
- What tone would you wish to establish for the scene?
- What movement around the stage would be worth mentioning?

Read the task again before you write your answer.